NORTH AMERICAN ANIMALS

Bighorn Sheep

by Megan Borgert-Spaniol

BLASTOFF! READERS

3

BELLWETHER MEDIA • MINNEAPOLIS, MN

Note to Librarians, Teachers, and Parents:

Blastoff! Readers are carefully developed by literacy experts and combine standards-based content with developmentally appropriate text.

Level 1 provides the most support through repetition of high-frequency words, light text, predictable sentence patterns, and strong visual support.

Level 2 offers early readers a bit more challenge through varied simple sentences, increased text load, and less repetition of high-frequency words.

Level 3 advances early-fluent readers toward fluency through increased text and concept load, less reliance on visuals, longer sentences, and more literary language.

Level 4 builds reading stamina by providing more text per page, increased use of punctuation, greater variation in sentence patterns, and increasingly challenging vocabulary.

Level 5 encourages children to move from "learning to read" to "reading to learn" by providing even more text, varied writing styles, and less familiar topics.

Whichever book is right for your reader, Blastoff! Readers are the perfect books to build confidence and encourage a love of reading that will last a lifetime!

This edition first published in 2016 by Bellwether Media, Inc.

No part of this publication may be reproduced in whole or in part without written permission of the publisher. For information regarding permission, write to Bellwether Media, Inc., Attention: Permissions Department, 5357 Penn Avenue South, Minneapolis, MN 55419.

Library of Congress Cataloging-in-Publication Data

Borgert-Spaniol, Megan, 1989- author.
Bighorn Sheep / by Megan Borgert-Spaniol.
    pages cm. – (Blastoff! Readers. North American Animals)
    Summary: "Simple text and full-color photography introduce beginning readers to bighorn sheep. Developed by literacy experts for students in kindergarten through third grade"– Provided by publisher.
    Audience: Ages 5-8
    Audience: K to grade 3
    Includes bibliographical references and index.
    ISBN 978-1-62617-257-9 (hardcover: alk. paper)
    1. Bighorn sheep–Juvenile literature. I. Title.
    QL737.U53B677 2016
    599.649'7–dc23
                                                    2015000518

Printed in the United States of America, North Mankato, MN.

Table of Contents

Bighorn sheep are hoofed **mammals**.

N
W E
S

Extinct

Extinct in the Wild

Critically Endangered

Endangered

Vulnerable

Near Threatened

Least Concern

bighorn sheep range =

conservation status: least concern

They can be found in western North America. Their range is between Canada and Mexico.

Bighorn sheep live in the mountains. They are at home in **foothills** and **alpine meadows**.

Some bighorn sheep are found in deserts.

Identify a Bighorn Sheep

white back end   curved horns   split hooves

Bighorn sheep climb and jump on steep, rocky slopes.

Split hooves help them balance. The hooves have soft bottoms that **grip** the rocks.

Grazing and Chewing

Bighorn sheep are **herbivores**. They eat grasses, **sedges**, and **shoots**. Those in deserts feed on cactuses and woody plants.

sagebrush

bear grass

rabbitbrush

desert holly

prickly pear cactuses

yellow sweet clover

The sheep **graze** throughout the day. After they eat, they find a safe place to chew their **cud**.

Male bighorn sheep are called **rams**. They have long, curled horns. The horns can weigh up to 30 pounds (13.6 kilograms).

Size of a Bighorn Sheep

average human

bighorn sheep

6
5
4
3
2
1
(feet)

Females are called **ewes**. They are smaller than rams. Their horns are shorter and straighter.

Animals to Avoid

coyotes

mountain lions

grizzly bears

gray wolves

bobcats

golden eagles

A ewe gives birth to a **lamb** on a high cliff. There it is safe from coyotes, mountain lions, and most other **predators**. However, it is an easy meal for a golden eagle.

Soon the lamb joins a **herd** with its mom. It climbs and plays with other young sheep. The lamb finds mom to drink her milk.

Baby Facts

Name for babies:	lambs
Size of litter:	1 lamb
Length of pregnancy:	5 to 6 months
Time spent with mom:	4 to 6 months

Most females stay in the
same herd for life.

Males leave the herd after a few years. They join smaller groups of rams.

Battle of the Rams

In fall, the largest rams fight for ewes.

Two rams charge each other.
Their horns crash together.
These battles can last for hours!

Glossary

alpine meadows—grassy fields that are found high up in mountains

cud—food that has been spit up to be chewed again

ewes—female bighorn sheep

foothills—hills at the base of a mountain

graze—to eat grasses and other plants on the ground

grip—to hold tightly

herbivores—animals that only eat plants

herd—a group of bighorn sheep

lamb—a baby bighorn sheep

mammals—warm-blooded animals that have backbones and feed their young milk

predators—animals that hunt other animals for food

rams—male bighorn sheep

sedges—grassy plants that grow in wet areas

shoots—plants that are just beginning to grow

split hooves—hooves that are split into two toes; hooves are hard coverings that protect the feet of some animals.

To Learn More

AT THE LIBRARY

Fraggalosch, Audrey. *Trails Above the Tree Line: A Story of a Rocky Mountain Meadow*. Norwalk, Conn.: Soundprints, 2002.

Kalman, Bobbie. *Baby Animals in Mountain Habitats*. New York, N.Y.: Crabtree Pub., 2011.

Macken, JoAnn Early. *Bighorn Sheep*. Pleasantville, N.Y.: Gareth Stevens Pub., 2010.

ON THE WEB

Learning more about bighorn sheep is as easy as 1, 2, 3.

1. Go to www.factsurfer.com.

2. Enter "bighorn sheep" into the search box.

3. Click the "Surf" button and you will see a list of related web sites.

With factsurfer.com, finding more information is just a click away.

Index

The images in this book are reproduced through the courtesy of: Tim Fitzharris/ Minden Pictures/ Corbis, front cover; Alexandra Demyanova, pp. 4-5; LaraBelova, pp. 6-7; Donald M. Jones/ Superstock, p. 7; David P. Lewis, p. 8 (top left); cpaulfell, p. 8 (top middle); karamysh, p. 8 (top right); Vinay A Bavdekar, p. 8 (bottom); Andrea Izzotti, p. 9; JeffGoulden, pp. 10-11; Kerry V. McQuaid, p. 11 (top left); NPS Photo/ Wikipedia, p. 11 (top right); Tim Pleasant, p. 11 (middle left); Rodney Mehring, p. 11 (middle right); Peter Zijlstra, p. 11 (bottom left); Benedictus, p. 11 (bottom right); Donald M. Jones/ Minden Pictures, pp. 12-13; Cynthia Kidwell, p. 14 (top left); Ultrashock, p. 14 (top right); Kane513, p. 14 (middle left); Maxim Kulko, p. 14 (middle right); Svetlana Foote, p. 14 (bottom left); withGod, p. 14 (bottom right); Don Johnston/ Glow Images, pp. 14-15; Robert McGouey/ Glow Images, pp. 16-17; BGSmith, p. 17; Tom Reichner, p. 18; Jared Hobbs/ Glow Images, pp. 18-19; Tom & Pat Leeson / a/ Age Fotostock, pp. 20-21.